THIS
BRAIN

The Imprisonment of Consciousness

How we serve time in Life, locked up in the prison of perception

JOSE VILLEGAS

Copyright ©2023

All rights reserved.
Permission to reproduce in any form
must be secured in writing
from the author.

ISBN: 9798325155581

Printed in the United States of America

Published May 2024

Contents

	Page
Introduction	v
How Did I Get Here?	1
The Brain	12
How the Brain Gets Developed	15
How to Change the Brain	21
Truths	22
Things to Practice to Help Change the Brain	25
We are Trapped by Ignorance and Knowledge	48
Understanding Our Reference for Truth	55
The Spiritual Tool of Going into Awareness	61
Why Does Going into Awareness Work?	65
The Devil is in Us	70
Be Nothing	74
We are the Created Creators	78
No Spiritual Order	81
The Physical World	88
Pain is a Gift	91
His Answers	93
Where are Our Answers?	96
We Bring Consciousness to the Physical World	100
We Can't Know what's Going to Happen Next	103
Things to Remember	106
Things we Should Know about Emotions	108
Things to Remember	112
Separation Talk	117
Where Would I Start?	119
Why is all of this Important?	121
Conclusion	123

Introduction

As I look out into the physical world today, it seems as if chaos and insanity are everywhere. Chaos and insanity aren't everywhere; they're only in one place, inside us as Human Beings. To be more accurate, they live in our brains and function through perception. Perception is how our brains perceive our physical experiences through the five senses and then release chemicals we feel as emotions and thoughts we think we are thinking.

As Human Beings, we have become the problem in the world today because of living through perception, but we are also the only solution because our "Wills" are free from everything, including the brain. Not even God, who created us, can make us do anything. That means we can love, hate, build, destroy, and give or take. What we see in the physical world today is the chaos and insanity within us being expressed. The physical world is the canvas for our feelings and thoughts. Our free "Will" is the brush that paints our physical reality through our daily decisions. How did we get to this place of chaos and insanity? Who's to blame? The reason we are in this place is because of the way God designed us as Human Beings. So, it's God's fault if there's a fault to be had because we did not create ourselves. When God created us, he gave the Being, which is us spiritually, a free "Will" but then put the brain in charge of the Human or physical body. And because we are in the body with the brain, it controls our physical lives without us knowing it. It had to be that way for us to survive the caveman stage of existence. In the beginning, God created a very dangerous and unforgiving planet and then created us on it. God could have created any kind of Earth he wanted, but He chose to create a dangerous and unforgiving one; why did he do that? Because when He created us, he sent us here without any information on how to be a Creator. So, he forced us into creating to know ourselves as Creators by putting us in survival mode, which caused us to develop weapons and medicines to save our physical lives. In prehistoric days, wild animals roamed the Earth freely, with the power to take our lives at any moment. To help us survive those dangers, the brain was created to automatically react to our physical experiences first without our permission. It did that by constantly scanning our physical environments for danger through the five senses. The goal of the brain was the survival of the organism, which was us. It did not need our conscious minds to participate. Because conscious thinking was too slow and contemplated to save us, the conscious mind would be thinking about what it heard and then try to come up with an answer before sending out the command to run. By then, it would be too late, and we would become their dinner. We needed something much quicker and more reactive than thinking, and that was the brain. It saved us from being prey so that we could evolve to the level of existence we live in today. But here's the problem with that setup. The brain is still reacting to life like a caveman in a spaceship society. The physical world has changed, but the brain is still functioning the same. What I see happening now is that the brain is still scanning our physical environments through the five senses for the new threats called pleasure, pain, sexism, and racism; the list of threats is endless. Today's new threats are not in the physical world but within us, and we have become a danger to each other. That's why we are doing mass shootings, trying to kill each other off like we did the wild animals. In the beginning, the brain saved us from the dangers of an undeveloped Planet, but now we need to be saved from it. God made the planet dangerous in the beginning, and now we are making it dangerous again. This time, it's not wild animals but us.

THE BRAIN

How Did I Get Here

How did I come to this place of understanding that it was my brain that was trapping me in the prison of perception for all the pain and suffering in my life? It was through practicing the 12 steps of Narcotics Anonymous. Of the 12 steps, three were pivotal in helping me see my prison of perception because everybody's prison is different. The three steps were the 4th, 5th, and 10th steps.

Let's start with the 4th step, which says, "We made a searching and fearless moral inventory of ourselves. The definition of morality says it is "concerned with the principles of right and wrong behavior and the goodness or badness of human character. This was the first time in my life that something introduced the concept of inventorying my morals. I wrote the 4th step as an autobiography. Writing down my life on paper allowed me to see things I did not know about myself. But writing it down didn't change it. It just made me aware of some of the things in my past. Writing a 4th step cannot reveal everything in one's past because there are layers on top of layers of behavior we must uncover.

This is where the 5th and 10th steps come into play. They helped me uncover things so I could discover them before recovering from the pain of my past. Even though my pain was created in the past, it was still alive in my present-moment experiences. That's because the brain creates mental and emotional reactions in the past that it uses to react to my physical experiences in the present moment. Because of that fact, the next step, the 5th step, was needed. The 5th step says, "We admitted to God, ourselves, and another human being the exact nature of our wrongs. I had to tell God, myself, and another human being about the exact nature of the wrongs I've done from the personal inventory that I wrote about in the 4th step. I decided to skip admitting to God or myself. I figured that if God is in every experience with me, then God already knows, and since I wrote it down, I now know, but another human being is the only one who doesn't know the exact nature of my wrongs. I didn't just talk about the wrongs I had done but the wrongs others had done to me as a child. I also talked about the wrongs I was still doing in the present moment. Talking to another Human Being about the wrongs I have done, what others have done to me, and the wrongs I was still doing was the

THE BRAIN

hardest part of the step, but it was also the most freeing. Because when someone else knows your story other than you, it takes the secrecy out of it. Because we are as sick as our secrets. The 5th step didn't say who the other Human Being had to be. Just tell somebody about the exact nature of your wrongs. At that time in my life, I didn't have a person I felt I could do that with because I had damaged the relationships with most of the people in my life because of my drug use. So, I started going around to NA meetings and telling the whole room the exact nature of my wrongs. For me, everybody in the room became another Human Being. Some people felt uncomfortable because I talked openly and honestly about my life. But it also caused others to openly talk about themselves after they heard me talk about myself. But because I paid more attention to the uncomfortable people, it almost made me stop talking about myself. I've always had this problem of wanting to be all right with everybody. That came from being bullied by this one guy in elementary which caused me to have a fear of people as an adult. I discovered this in the fourth step when I wrote about my past experiences. I could have 98 people out of a hundred say that they liked what I said, and two didn't; I would focus on the 2. I know that you can't make everybody happy or that everybody will like you.

But when needing everybody to like you shows up as an emotion, it is hard to catch, and that emotion will drive you to try to get everybody to like you. But I kept talking about my past and daily experiences because I wanted to change my life. I wanted more than just not using drugs. I wanted to change the life that made using drugs ok. And because I went to meetings daily and talked about my wrongs, I was actually doing the 10th step but didn't know it. Here's what the 10th step says, and I quote, "We continued to take personal inventory, and when we were wrong, we promptly admitted it. What it is saying is that I must continually watch my behavior and, when I'm wrong, promptly admit it to someone. Promptly means, with little or no delay, immediately. Here's why those three steps were pivotal in changing my life. They helped me to see how my past was trapping me spiritually in the present moment. Writing the 4th step down on paper allowed me to see my past. Doing the 5th step made me comfortable talking about my past to another Human Being. The 10th step gave me something to practice daily to notice my past in my present-moment experiences. Out of the three steps, the 10th step was the most important. Here's why? The 10th step called for me to monitor my behavior throughout the day, and when I noticed something wrong, I had to tell someone. Remember that the brain is reacting

THE BRAIN

to all our physical experiences from the past. I needed something to practice that helped me to notice my past in the present moment, and that's what the 10th step gave me. I became aware of my past because of telling someone else, which made me start to notice it when it showed up. That awareness caused me to make different decisions in the present moment to my past experiences. That's when I noticed that my past was weakening from the different decisions I made in the present moment. The past must be changed in the present moment. Because that's where it's showing up as perception. The 10th step, if practiced, encompasses both the 4th and 5th steps. The 4th step is an inventory of my past experiences. The 5th step is telling someone, and the 10th step is both. The big difference is that you must practice the 10th step throughout the day all day. Now, here's the part of my story where my life started to change because of practicing the 10th step. One day, while speaking at an NA Convention in Pittsburg, PA, I met a brother named Robert Shakhan. Rob lived in Detroit, MI, and I lived in Washington, DC. We lived over 500 miles away but talked daily as if we lived next door. That day at the NA Convention, I gave my number to many people after I spoke, but Rob was the only one who called me. The first time we talked, it was as if we had been friends for a long time; our stories were so similar that it was easy for us to communicate. Rob became that other Human Being to whom I also admitted the exact nature of my wrongs. And I became that for him. I believe Rob came into my life so that I could practice the 10th step all the time without waiting until I went to an NA meeting. Because the only time I talked about myself was at an NA meeting. And waiting until I went to an NA meeting might be too far away from the experience I needed to discuss. I might not remember the exact nature of my wrongs from earlier that day. Or what if I didn't go to an NA meeting that day? I wouldn't get to talk about anything I noticed about my life that day. By meeting Rob, life was showing me that to change, I needed to talk about my wrongs as they were happening. That is the part in the 10th step where it says to promptly admit it. I didn't have to talk about them right when they happened but at some point, that day. Rob and I would talk to each other multiple times on the same day about our lives. As Rob and I talked daily, we didn't realize that we were doing the 10th step with each other. To us, we were just talking about the things we noticed about ourselves and others in our physical lives. And we didn't just talk about the exact nature of our wrongs but our fears. It wasn't until I started talking about my fears that I realized that I lived in some form of fear most of the time. It wasn't

THE BRAIN

physical fear like being physically scared of someone. It was more emotional fear. Like not wanting anybody to get mad at me for something I said or did. So, I would keep letting things go until people considered me a pushover. Or scared to ask for anything I wanted. It didn't matter if it was my wife, our kids, my co-workers, or the supervisor at work; the fear was the same. I remember talking to Rob about my fear of asking for a day off. The fear came from listening to the supervisor earlier that day fuss about how others were missing work, so I didn't want him to be mad at me for asking for a day off that I needed to take. Can you see how that fear created in my childhood of not wanting anyone to be mad at me for asking for what I wanted was still driving my decisions? But after talking to Rob about it, I realized that it was fear being released into my body by my brain and not the truth, so I asked for the day off and got it. It was fear and not the truth because I had not asked for the day off yet. Rob and I talked about everything many times during the day. We came up with this saying that we would say to each other when we talked, "Put it in the physical." Here's how we used it in our conversations. Rob would call me and talk about how he felt about a physical experience he had just had, and I would say, "Put it in the Physical." That meant re-telling the entire physical experience that made him feel that way so we could fully understand how his brain was perceiving the experience. It would be the same when I called him. Over time, we started our conversations off with "Putting it in the physical" without anyone asking. Could you imagine how much you would learn about your life if you talked about yourself in that way daily? To be more precise, how much would you learn about the kind of brain you are living with that's trapping you behind the veil of perception? Here's an example of "Putting it in the physical" when Rob and I talked. One day, I called Rob to talk about an experience I had just had at Chipotle and what I noticed. Here's the experience and what I noticed inside of me. While waiting to be served, I noticed that the young lady fixing the bowls kept fixing the mobile orders as if no one was standing in line. That's when the cashier bought her another mobile order, and she started fixing it. At that moment, I decided to say something. That's when I noticed that my stomach began to turn like it was upset. I decided to speak up anyway, regardless of how I felt. I asked to speak to the manager, and the issue was resolved. I asked Rob why my stomach was feeling upset. Before he could say anything, it hit me, and I said it was because I was going against that nice guy who doesn't like people being mad at him. It was a physical reality that my brain wanted me to keep

THE BRAIN

living. The upset stomach came from my brain releasing chemicals into my body to try and control my decision. It did that by making me feel nervous when I got ready to speak up for myself. This is how Rob and I talked to each other about ourselves. That experience also taught me that learning about how our brains control us through emotions and thoughts can't be learned from a book. It must be discovered in our own physical experiences. The brain reacts to our physical experiences based on how it was developed, not something we read. I realized that the brain operating through perception doesn't care if the decision is big or small; it wants total control of our lives and uses chemicals we call emotions and thoughts we think we are thinking. And the only way to catch the brain is to start practicing talking about how it makes you feel and think inside of different experiences. This works because you will become aware of your feelings and thoughts before you act. Everybody talks or texts someone daily, but they usually talk about others. Never about themselves and how their physical experiences make them feel and think. Talking about our physical experiences at the mental and emotional levels helps us to understand ourselves and others. Here are some things I've discovered about myself that I did not know because of talking to Rob about my life. I did not know that

I was addicted to security; I needed to have a job all the time, even though I knew I had this message that the world needed to hear. That need for security would not allow me to go all in and step out with the faith that everything would be all right. Something else I didn't know about myself was that I complained a lot, most of the time. It wasn't until I told Rob about it that I began to work on it in my daily experiences. When I noticed myself doing it, I would stop talking. Another was that I was a pessimist, acting like an optimist. I was acting like a nice person who was angry a lot. Finally, I would dominate the conversation when talking to others. I realized that I talked too much. Because of that realization, I started going into discussions with others with the intent of listening more. I'm not the only one with this problem. Most of us are talking or texting too much. These are just a few things I've discovered about myself that I did not know. That's when I realized that you can be with yourself all day and not know yourself, or shall I say, the kind of brain you're living with through perception. The brain operating through perception won't allow you to see your behavior, only the behavior of others. It makes you think the problem is always outside of you, not in you. The most important discovery a person can make is to discover what kind of brain they live with.

THE BRAIN

That must be done through your physical experiences in the present moment. I discovered that I was living with a brain that did not like me. Imagine living with something controlling your physical life that's not on your side. This book is about helping you understand the brain's workings and getting it on your side. To do that, I first must define the brain, then show how it is developed, and lastly, how to change it.

The Brain

It's an organ of soft nervous tissue contained in the skull of vertebrates, functioning as the coordinating center of sensation, intellect, and nervous activity. That means it coordinates what we feel, think, and how we physically move.

Let's define the functions that the brain coordinates. Let's start with "Sensation". Sensation is a physical feeling or perception resulting from something that happens to or comes into contact with the physical body. Let's also define the word perception in the definition of sensation. It is the ability to see, hear, or become aware of something through the 5 senses. So, there are two ways that sensation is stimulated inside of us. The first way is when something comes into contact with our physical bodies. And the second is through the 5 senses. Now, let's define another function that the brain coordinates and that is the intellect. Intellect- is the faculty of reasoning and understanding objectively, especially regarding abstract or academic matters. Objectivity is defined as seeing things in a way that is not influenced by our personal feelings or opinions. Let's also define its

THE BRAIN

opposite, which is subjectivity. Subjective is to see things in a way that is based on our own personal feelings, tastes, or opinions. So, the intellect or the mind is supposed to reason objectively but doesn't. It reasons more subjectively. The mind doesn't objectively see things in our physical experiences because our feelings and opinions always influence it. And with the invention of social media, people are more subjective than ever before. Our intellect always takes a side in our physical experiences, making it subjective and closed-minded. You can see it everywhere, with all the groups vying for power and control over each other. Now, let's define the last part of the definition of the brain, which is nervous activity. Nervous activity is the nerves in motion. Nerves are defined as a whitish fiber or bundle of fibers that transmits impulses of sensation to the spinal cord and brain and impulses from them to the muscles and organs. There's that word again, "sensation." Sensations are only transmitted through the nerves when something comes into contact with the body. The nerves are the transmission lines of sensations to the spinal cord and brain. Then, the brain sends an impulse to the muscles and organs. We need more blood and oxygen to act, so it shuts down body parts not required right now to send more blood to the heart and generate more oxygen from the lungs. This is why continuous stress makes us physically sick and eventually kills us because of constantly shutting down body parts that are needed. Nerves connect the body, brain, and the physical world. Now that I've defined the brain, let's talk about how it gets developed.

THE BRAIN

How the Brain Gets Developed

The brain is defined as the coordinating center of sensation, intellect, and nervous activity. But before it can coordinate, it must first be developed by our physical environments to know how to coordinate our physical lives. The brain doesn't judge our physical environments as being good or bad, right or wrong; it just coordinates how we feel, think, and act after it's developed. And because it coordinates how we feel, think, and act, it controls our physical lives.

By controlling our physical lives, it controls us but doesn't have control over us. Meaning it can't make us do anything. The only reason it controls us is because of ignorance about how it works. If you grew up around winning, losing, racism, sexism, love, or hate, your brain will coordinate your physical life to reflect that information. The brain is one of God's most powerful creations and is the least understood. In today's world, understanding the brain is of utmost importance. All the craziness we see in the world today is the brain, not the devil. So, how is the brain developed? It is developed at the beginning of our lives as babies through sensations. Remember what the definition of sensation is. Anything that comes into contact with the physical body or is perceived through the 5 senses. But why must the brain be developed through sensations? It's because the brain is inside the physical body and not in the physical world, so it can't experience the physical world as physical. And because we are in the body, we must also experience the physical world as sensations. That means all our physical experiences are transformed into sensations and then transmitted to the brain for development. How do you know if something is hard or soft? By how it feels, and that is a sensation and not a thing. The tree is hard, the door is hard, and the concrete sidewalk is hard. I just described three things with the same sensation, but the sensation did not describe the thing, just how it felt. There's a sensation for soft, hot, cold, warm, and sunny, to name a few. We must understand that the physical world must be experienced as sensations. While sensations are developing the brain, the brain is creating mental and emotional reactions to the sensations. Say someone as a child doesn't like peas; how the peas taste is a sensation, then the brain creates a reaction to peas. Mommy puts peas on their plate, and they react by crying until Mommy threatens them with a belt to eat the peas. You might think the peas created the reaction but didn't because they are neutral. The peas don't care if you like them or not; they are just peas. The taste buds and the brain decided if the child likes peas, and the child accepts it as the truth about peas. I used this example to show that this happens with everything; our lives are defined for us but not by us. It's done through sensations, the five senses, and the brain. Once the brain is developed enough by sensations, it moves into power over us by reacting to incoming sensations. Then, we go from a sensation-driven life as a child to a reactional one as an adult. This is how the brain controls our physical lives and traps us in the prison of perception. What's the difference between a sensation and an emotion? Sensations are how the physical world feels, tastes, smells, looks, and sounds; an emotion is a chemical released from our brains in reaction to sensations. Love, anger, and frustration are emotions and not sensations. The outer world creates sensations, and emotions come from the brain that lives in the inner world. God created physical sensations as a way for us to spiritually experience matter. As Human Beings, we live in both worlds simultaneously, and sensation is how we spiritually experience the physical world through the body. But how does sensation reach the brain to develop it? It's through the nerves, the five senses, and the spinal cord. Let's start with the nerves. Every part of our bodies has nerves; that's because the brain is not connected to every part of our bodies; it is only connected to the spinal cord, where all the nerves come together from all body parts. That's why the spinal cord is defined as the central nervous system. The spinal cord is like the union station for nerves, where all the nerves come together. Nerves are the means of transportation of sensation when something comes into contact with the physical body. Say, for example, you hit your toe on the edge of the bed; that pain was sent through a nerve in your toe to the spinal cord, and the spinal cord then sent it to the brain. The brain then sends back an impulse to the sensation of pain that either makes you holler or stop and bend over until the pain subsides. That's a sensation created by physical contact. The other way sensation develops the brain is through perception, and perception is anything perceived through the 5 senses. It's actually the four senses minus touch. The whole body is created for touch. However, the other four senses are the most powerful way sensation develops the brain and how we learn. When sensation comes in through the four senses, the nerves don't need to transmit it because they are connected directly to the brain. Have you ever noticed that your eyes, ears, nose, and mouth are all up on your head where your brain is? The brain only uses the central nervous system to transmit impulses to our muscles and organs when something is perceived. Many new diseases today will not show up on a brain scan because we need

THE BRAIN

to be in the physical experience to cause the brain to release the chemicals that are making us sick. Here's an example of how our physical experiences cause our brains to release chemicals that control us. Say you are walking home alone at night and hear something coming from a dark alley. That sound is sent to the brain through the ears, and then the brain releases emotions that cause an impulse that prepares you to fight or flight. This process is done for you by the sensation of sound coming in through the ears and into the brain. The only part we play in it is what decision we will make, to fight or flight. The emotion the brain releases into our bodies will either make us stronger for fighting or fearful for flight; we have no control over that. Another critical understanding of sensations is that when we learn through the four senses, they must come with information and instructions. That's why, as a child, we use flashcards to teach us about things in the physical world first. For example, we must first learn what a police car looks like. Then, as a child, while riding in the car, a police car drives by with its siren blaring. Someone in the car might say that you must pull over and let them by when you hear that sound. That's sensations with information and instructions. But there's another way that sensations develop the brain but don't come with flashcards. They are behavioral sensations created by watching others. There aren't any flashcards for winners, losers, sexists, or racists because it's demonstrated by the people in our physical environments. Behavioral sensations come with the information and instructions together as you are experiencing them as a child. So, let me sum it all up about the power of sensations and how they develop us. The brain must be developed by sensations coming in from our physical environments because it's not in the physical world but in the physical body. Sensations are generated in us in two ways: through physical contact or perceived through the four senses. Sensations perceived through the four senses must contain information about the sensations and instructions on what to do when they happen. Sensations observed through other's behavior don't have flashcards to describe them because they come with information and instruction. Why is all this important? Because our spiritual freedom is at stake on Earth, we must understand that we are chasing sensations, not things. That's why we are constantly buying more things to feel satisfied. The physical world can't satisfy us because the brain continually changes the chemicals it releases in reaction to sensations. Now, let's talk about how to change our brains because life becomes much easier if our brains are on our side.

THE BRAIN

How to Change the Brain

Everything I've learned about changing my life was done outside my daily activities. When I meditated or prayed, it was done in a quiet place away from my daily activities. When I went to church or my NA and AA meetings, I left my daily activities to sit and listen to others talk about change.

I'm not telling you to stop doing any of these things because they all are a part of changing your life. What I'm talking about is what to do when you're not doing those things. When you return to your daily activities after meditation or prayer or leaving your place of worship or the NA and AA meetings. It's in our daily activities where the brain is controlling us through perception. The brain must be changed in our daily activities. So, how do we change our brains? Let's start with some truths about the brain, then something to practice that will alter how it reacts.

Truths

- The first truth is that once the brain is developed by our physical experiences as a child, it can't change itself. That means we have something inside of us that's running our physical lives that can't change itself, even when the information it uses hurts us. The brain can be changed; it just can't do it. Why can't it change itself? It's because it can't be still once it's developed. It must react to all our physical experiences. And without the ability to be still, it can't learn anything about how it's reacting. Remember that the brain was created to be reactional, not observational. It must react to everything coming through the five senses.

- We can't create any emotions; that's the brain's job. We can only stimulate them. Emotions are not feelings but chemicals that we feel. Emotions are a physical illusion, just like time. A physical illusion is when something makes us think it's something else. Emotions make you believe they are feelings, but they are not; they are chemicals we feel. That's why we can treat mental and emotional disorders with physical medicine. They are treating the brain by trying to control the chemicals it releases. Because emotions are chemicals that we feel, I now understand how addiction happens. It's when a person constantly tries to stimulate the same chemicals in their brain.

- This truth is fundamental and vital. The brain doesn't know the difference between something you are thinking about and an actual physical experience. It will release the same emotional chemicals. That's why we wake up from nightmares. We feel the fear as if the dream was physically real. The brain can't distinguish between an actual physical experience and a dream. That's because the brain is a reactor and not an observer. It's only looking to be stimulated by the physical world, not to distinguish the differences. I believe that what we are calling the past is a bunch of emotional reactions controlled by the brain, waiting to be stimulated by our physical experiences in the present moment. This is why so many people are making themselves physically sick from thought alone. Because the brain will react to a thought of stress as if it were real stress and release the same organ-destroying chemicals.

- Because of the preceding truth that the brain doesn't know the difference between something we are thinking about and something we are physically experiencing, we can create a better life for ourselves by selecting the thoughts of what we want and acting like we have received it, which will make the brain release the chemicals that will draw it to us. Thought alone is not as powerful as a thought energized by an emotion. But we must also align our actions to what we want. Not aligning our actions to what we want is like traveling to New York but heading towards North Carolina. We are heading the wrong way to our desires.

THE BRAIN

Things to Practice to Help Change the Brain

1. We must use our free "Will" to free us from our brains. The brain can't make us do anything. But it does have the power to influence our decisions. It does that by releasing chemicals that we feel and thoughts we think we are thinking. It's not personal; it's reactional. This happens to us all, every moment of the day. It doesn't matter if you live as a Christian, Muslim, Buddhist, or even an Atheist; this process is the same for everybody, and nobody is getting out of it. So, what do we practice to free ourselves from perception? We must practice not reacting unconsciously to perception in the present moment. That means we must stop reacting

to our feelings and thoughts so quickly. What's a reaction? It's a quick decision. And unconscious means we do it without thinking. I would start the practice of slowing my reaction down to any negative state. A negative state is any feelings or thoughts that you don't like. That includes anger, frustration, sadness, and hatred, to name a few states. I would practice hesitating and observing when I felt an emotion or thought I didn't like. I would practice not wearing how I felt on my face and in my body movements. We can act differently than how we feel. For example, if I don't feel like going to work, I act more upbeat until the emotion catches up with the acting. Emotions can't control you if you don't attach yourself to them. We attach ourselves to a feeling by making unconscious decisions based on how we feel now. Say you are someone who, when you feel anger and get mad, loses control and gets violent. You would have to practice hesitating by letting some stuff go and allowing the feeling to return to normal. You may have to remove yourself from the physical experience to not let the emotion build to the level of losing control. But why does this work? When we don't react, it chips away at the emotional reaction in the brain until it stops showing up as strong in our physical experience. Our power to help our brains change lies in the power of our free "Will." That's why we can change our lives by just making different decisions. Nothing stays the same if the decision that supports it changes.

2. I came up with a practice called "Let's just wait and see". "Let's just wait and see" is one of the most powerful ways to separate from our brains. Why is it so powerful? Because it keeps us in observation mode by not reacting so quickly to what we feel and think. When we tell our brains, "Let's just wait and see," it slowly takes perception out of the driver's

seat of our lives. It also dissolves the emotional reactions that the brain has created in reaction to sensations. The brain loves to run our lives by trying to be God. It does that by telling us what will happen next when it doesn't know what will happen next until it happens. Only God knows what will happen next before it happens and communicates that directly to us before it happens. That voice we call "something said" is God communicating with us. But God can only tell us what will happen next; he can't stop us from doing whatever we want, including ignoring him. We have the power of choice; using that power correctly is how we separate from the brain that controls us through perception. The brain has what I call a reactive free "Will," meaning that it must react to all our physical experiences and can't be still to observe what's happening. And because its "Will" is reactive, it also means that we can't stop it from reacting. Telling the brain, "Let's just wait and see," keeps us in the moment. The reason "Let's just wait and see" is so powerful is because it allows the brain to have its reaction. It helps us to stop reacting to it so quickly. Practicing "Let's just wait and see" doesn't fight against what the brain perceives. Remember how the brain reacts to our physical experiences. It's either a feeling or thought or both. Here's a real-life example of what it looks like in my physical experiences. One day, I decided that I was going to go downtown to DC, and I live in Maryland. It was a little past noon, and as soon as I decided to go to DC, my brain reacted to that decision through thought alone as my mind. It immediately started talking about how much traffic it would be if I went now. It went on and on about how I wouldn't find a parking space at this time of day. I calmly listened to what my brain had to say and then said to it, "Let's just wait and see," for the first time in a long time, my brain fell into silence. The reason it stopped talking was because it had nowhere to go. I didn't react to its opinion or say that it was wrong. I didn't fight or ignore it. I did not try to suppress it or push what it said out of my consciousness. By telling my brain, "Let's just wait and see," I took it out of the leadership role and put it in the servant role. What is happening is that I'm letting my physical experiences lead and not my brain. When we let our physical experiences lead, we won't be misled. That doesn't mean you can't plan to have an experience. It just means you can't plan how that experience will turn out. How did the earlier experience with going downtown turn out? First, there wasn't any traffic, and I got a parking space right in front of the building I was going to. What if it had been traffic and I did not get a parking space in front of the building I was going to? It was never about the traffic or parking but about becoming aware of how

THE BRAIN

our brains are trying to run our lives by telling us what will happen before it happens. I gave this example at one of my seminars, and a gentleman raised his hand and asked if it wouldn't be common sense at that time of the day that there would be traffic. I told him this is not about common sense but realizing that our brains acting through perception can't know something that hasn't happened yet. How can my brain know what's happening in DC while I'm still standing in my living room in Maryland? It can't because it can only know what the five senses know. Sometimes, it can guess and get it right, but a broken clock is right twice a day. When I tell my brain, "Let's just wait and see," it automatically creates separation from it. Because I'm the talker and not the listener. Usually, I'm the listener who unconsciously reacts to the talker, which is the brain. When I'm talking to my brain, I'm doing it from within my body and not with my mouth, so only I know what I'm saying to it, and boy, what freedom from perception I have today. When I think about an experience that hasn't happened yet but is going to happen and my brain tries to tell me what's going to happen, I tell it, "Let's just wait and see." In the beginning, you will have to think about doing it because it is not a habit yet, but once it becomes a habit where you do it without thinking, your physical life will change. I did not say it might change, but it will change. It will change because our physical world is just a reflection of our choices. If we make decisions based on the brain's perception, we will keep creating our childhoods in adulthood. When we practice telling the brain, "Let's just wait and see," we are not deciding from what it knows. This is why your physical life must change; your decisions are different. You can start today by practicing telling your brain, "Let's just wait and see," and you will be amazed at how wrong your brain is most of the time. "Let's just wait and see" helps us to make freer decisions. Now let's move on to the companion of "Let's just wait and see," which is "Let's go and see."

3. What's the difference between "Let's just wait and see" and "Let's go and see"? It's fear. One has more fear, and the other doesn't. "Let's just wait and see" is more mental, where the brain tells me what will happen. "Let's go and see" is more emotional because my brain releases emotions that react to my physical experiences before I decide. Here's a real-life example so that you can understand how it feels. I give real-life examples because you can't benefit from this understanding if you can't catch it in your own physical experiences. One day, I walked into my usual barbershop to get a haircut, and the barber who usually cuts my hair had three people waiting for a cut. At that moment, I decided I didn't want to wait 2 hours for

a haircut. Then I noticed that the barber beside him had no one in his chair. As I was thinking about what I wanted to do, I decided that I was going to ask the barber who had nobody to cut my hair. The moment I decided to ask the other barber to cut my hair, fear came over me. Notice that I haven't asked the barber yet; I just thought about what I wanted to do. My brain released chemicals into my body that made me fearful to do what I wanted. Then, my mind reacted by saying that the barber I usually use would get mad if I asked the other barber to cut my hair. No one around me knows that I'm going through this over a haircut because I'm going through it from within my body where I spiritually am. At that moment, I said to my brain, "Let's go and see" if what you say is true. I then went over to the other barber, still feeling the fear, and asked him to cut my hair. At the end of my haircut, not only did the barber I usually used not

THE BRAIN

get mad, but he didn't even realize I was gone. If I had listened to my brain, I would have sat there for 2 hours because of fear of the other barber getting mad. It's important to understand that the fear was trying to stop me from deciding, and my brain started telling me a story about what it thought would happen. But because of practicing "Let's go and see," I've created enough separation from my brain to see the truth in the physical experience. It's not our brain's fault for trying to run our lives because we were attached to it as babies, and there has never been any information that detaches us from it. We are so connected to the brain that we believe we are the brain. This is not about having power or control over the brain but about having power and control over us.

4. We must practice being still while in our daily activities. It's easy to practice being still in prayer or meditation, but can you do it

when everything around you is moving? When you get up from prayer or meditation and return to your daily activities, practice not reacting so quickly to your feelings and thoughts. If we are not reacting, we are observing; observing is inner stillness. Deciding not to react creates stillness, and choosing to act creates movement.

5. We must practice using our imagination. The only time I've ever heard the word imagination talked about was in some fairy tale like Alice in Wonderland. But imagination is a part of who we are; it's only an ability given to us. Animals can't imagine being anything else because they were not created to be Creators. As Creators, we must see the idea before we create it. Imagination works because the brain doesn't know the difference between an experience happening now and one only imagined. Look at the word imagination. Image-in-

THE BRAIN

nation. We hold the image of what we want and act as if we have it already until it shows up in the nation or physical world. However, the key to using imagination is to act like we have received what we imagine. Sometimes, you don't feel it, but keep acting like you have it, and the feeling will catch up with the acting. The brain was created for our physical survival; it doesn't know how to create from imagination or the unseen world. The brain can't imagine a different outcome in our physical experiences because it uses our past experiences to react in the present moment. The physical world controls the brain through the five senses. That process is called perception. Imagination operates outside of the five senses. We are the only ones on the earth with that ability. Our brains will react to what we imagine by going against it with physical reality. It will try to keep us focused on the things already here, not what we want to create through imagination. To use imagination, we must understand that the physical life we are now living is not the only reality. We are the only ones on the earth who can imagine a different outcome, but because we're not taught how to create from imagination, we live through the brain in survival mode all the time and don't know it. We are still living in survival mode today as Human Beings. There are only two ways we create: survival and imagination. Creating through survival mode puts the brain in charge of what we create, and creating through imagination puts us in charge. I don't just use my imagination for big things; I use it daily. Here's how I use it. My wife and I are landlords and one day, I got a call from one of the tenants that the AC stopped working. The first chemical that my brain released into my body was the feeling of frustration with the property from all the past frustrations. Operating as the mind, the brain says, "If it's not one thing, it's another."

Because I've been practicing using my imagination in my daily experiences. I decided to imagine the outcome I wanted to see in that experience. So, I let go of the feeling of frustration and the thought that if it's not one thing, it's another. I replaced that thought with the thought that everything I needed would come to me. Then, I watched the universe move in my favor and brought everything I needed to solve the problem without much effort on my part. Imagination is a powerful gift given only to us. We must stop letting it go unused or misused.

6. We must feed ourselves good information until we stop forgetting who we are. Who are we? We are Creators who can use the brain to create the life we want. I see people on their cell phones all day, yet they don't download any good information about themselves into their memory. The smartphone can help you to change your brain or keep

it the same. The problem with social media is that it allows you to be in everybody else's business but your own. That's why they call us followers and not leaders. If you are going to follow somebody, they should at least help you to change your life. Because of the smartphone and the internet, I have bought books and listened to information I otherwise would not have known existed; people like Neville Goddard, born in 1905, have written many books. Dr. Joe Dispenza wrote "Breaking the Habit of Being Yourself" and many other books. Dr. Bruce Lipton who authored "The Biography of Beliefs" and Candace Pert's book, the "Molecules of Emotions." These are just a few of the people I listen to on YouTube on my smartphone while at the gym or work. I seek new information to put new thoughts in my brain. Until we download some new and different information, the thoughts we have to select from will be limited.

THE BRAIN

7. We must stop watching the news every day. We can't get away from all news unless we disconnect from all devices. But we can limit how much of it we download into our brains. The news can become an addiction without us knowing it. The news is one-sided. That side is negative. And because it's negative, it shapes our opinion of others and the physical world. Because it negatively shapes our opinion, we are contributing to the negativity the world is in through our emotions and thoughts.

8. We must practice not dragging negative emotions around all day. Let them go the moment you notice that you are holding on to them. How would you know? Notice how you feel and act. See if you are still irritated or frustrated. Act positive and watch how the emotion catches up with it later.

9. We must work on "using." The word "using" was introduced to me when I became a member of Narcotics Anonymous. You would

hear someone say I didn't "use" today. What they were talking about is that they didn't use drugs or drink alcohol to change how they felt, just for today. Then one day, I realized that I had stopped smoking crack cocaine, but I didn't quit "using." Meaning I was still using other things to make myself feel good, like sex, people-pleasing, and food. I was even using Church to feel good. Nothing got me more emotionally high than the praise and worship part of the service. It's important to understand that drugs didn't make me high, nor did food, people-pleasing, or the praise and worship part of the church service. What they all did was cause my brain to release the chemicals that made me feel good. Our brains come with chemicals that we call emotions that make us feel good, bad, and everything else in between. Let me show you how the brain works. One day, I'm watching the movie Elvis, and a scene comes on where he's a little boy who sees a tent with a lot of

THE BRAIN

singing and shouting; he goes into this tent where they are having a church revival. While looking at the scene, I felt the hairs on my arms stand up, and a wave came over my body that made me feel good. That's when I realized that my brain was also experiencing the movie and released chemicals into my body that made the hairs on my arms stand up and that wave of good feelings. This is how the brain controls us without our knowledge of it happening. But once we understand this process, we can use it to change our lives. For example, I play gospel music when I go to the gym. That's because it causes my brain to release feel-good chemicals that push me for another 20 minutes on the treadmill. I'm using something in the physical world to stimulate the chemical release I want from the brain.

10. We must stop seeking only pleasure while avoiding pain. Pleasure is a never-ending

cycle, and pain is usually a new beginning. There will never be enough pleasure to keep us happy all the time. Pleasure can't keep us happy because it will eventually stop working as it initially did. Have you ever enjoyed an experience and then did it again but couldn't capture that same feeling? That's because the brain changes how it feels about the experience and releases different chemicals into our bodies. But pain, if we are ready, can lead to significant changes in our lives.

11. We must catch ourselves unconsciously doing the behaviors we are trying to change. When I started working on people-pleasing, I had to catch myself doing it in my physical experiences. The more I practice catching myself people-pleasing, the easier it got to catch it. This is where most stay stuck because they work on themselves away from their daily experiences and then go back into their daily experiences

and react unconsciously to what they are trying to change.

12. An addiction to a substance is much easier to stop than an addictive behavior. That's because the longer we stop doing the substance, the easier it becomes to stay stopped. But the behavior is being used constantly, so it is harder to stop doing it. It also has emotions and thoughts on its side. The preceding step is crucial because you must catch yourself doing the behavior you are trying to stop. It will be challenging initially because you will have to think about catching it, but if you do it until it becomes a habit, the habit will do it on its own without you thinking about it.

13. We must be working full-time on separation from our brains. Our brains are all in when it comes to controlling us through perception. The work to separate us from perception must be done in the present moment, one physical

experience at a time. But we must be committed to doing it full-time, not part-time. We must be on in.

14. Put up reminders to remind you of what you are working on. I would take a business card, write "Separation from Perception" on the back, and tape it on my computer. Some days, just seeing that card would wake me up from unconscious thinking.

15. We must stop falling for the value trap. The value trap is when we give things more value than people. We then buy a whole lot of expensive stuff in an attempt to feel valuable. The only ones on the Earth who can give and take away value are us, but because we don't know it, we seek self-worth through things. Take, for example, a five-dollar bill doesn't know that it is less than a ten-dollar bill, that's because they can give themselves value. We are the only value givers on the Earth and must start to value each other if we

THE BRAIN

want the world to get better. That includes giving yourself value. Stop giving your things more value than your health.

JOSE VILLEGAS

We are Trapped by Ignorance and Knowledge

First, let me talk about ignorance and how it traps us. We are the most powerful entity on Earth, but we don't know it when we are born. God created us as Creators to run the physical world but sent us here without any instructions on how to do it. Would you give someone such an important job as running the physical world and not instruct them on how to do it? No, you wouldn't. Well, that's what God did to us. He created us to do the most important job on Earth but sent us here in total ignorance.

Ignorance doesn't mean we are dumb or stupid. It just means we don't know anything. When I say anything, I mean nothing. We're so ignorant that we don't know anything about the earth or who we are on it. We don't know what anything is called. That's why we use flashcards to teach us about things in the physical world. And because we enter the physical world in total ignorance of everything, including ourselves, it sets

THE BRAIN

us up to be spiritually controlled by physical information. How does physical information control us spiritually? It's because we don't have any reference for the truth. We don't know if what we are learning is true or not. All information coming in from our physical environments as children is true to us until proven not. If you were taught that the light switch was called a door, and the door was called a light switch, you would have to believe it. Because you don't know what either is. I now understand why it says in the Bible, "Lean not to your understanding." We didn't create our own understanding; it was created for us by the physical environment we grew up in. But why did God send us here in that condition? For us to be Creators, all creative options must be available. We must be able to look at everything in the physical world and think of a better or different way of doing it. If not another way, create a whole new way. As Creators, we must be able to see the future before we create it. If we entered the earth already programmed, it would create spiritual blindness in our awareness of what we can see in our physical experiences. However, because of the information we get after we get here, we become unconscious of any other options in our lives. That's why it is important to separate from perception so that we can see and create a different life for ourselves. But there's an important reason for entering the physical world in a state of total ignorance. It allows evolution to be in charge of what and when something gets created on the earth, not us. What is evolution? It's when the earth has evolved enough that the next creative idea appears in somebody's mind. Here's what I mean about evolution being in charge and not us. What if life had revealed electricity to the caveman while he was still living in a cave? What was he going to do with that idea? Light up his cave. That wouldn't be possible because electrical wires or lights had not been invented yet. The earth had not evolved enough to where electricity was needed yet. The caveman's ignorance would not allow him to see the possibility of electricity in the lightning until the earth was ready to use it. When the earth was ready for electricity, a Creator was born that could see electricity in the lightning. Ignorance doesn't allow ideas to enter the earth out of place. The earth always sets the stage for the next thing to be created, and it's our job to see it and then create it. As Creators, our main job here on the earth is to turn ideas into things. Everything on the earth was an idea first before it became a thing. We are the connection between the physical and spiritual worlds. Now that I've talked about ignorance, let's talk about how knowledge locks us up in the prison of perception. Knowledge traps us because it lacks information about us that we need to be powerful on Earth. Even when I went to church as a child,

THE BRAIN

they never taught me anything about having any power but how worthless I was in the eyes of God. They used to say we were all no-good sinners, only saved by grace. Some would even go as far as calling themselves filthy rags. We would sing songs about how no-good we were and how good God was. It's important to understand that when we download information from our physical environments as a child, we can't challenge it or even know if it's true. Once downloaded, it becomes a part of perception and is controlled by the brain. We all must download a software program or operating system from our physical environments as a child. Nobody can get around this process, and everyone must go through it. That means everybody is programmed. Most of the information we download creates unconsciousness, turning us into robots with free "Will." Think about it momentarily. Your life is based on the download you downloaded as a child, which you followed unconsciously. We are not taught that that first download as a child should not be the last one in our lives. But most of us are still living from that first download of information as children in today's world as adults. That's like trying to use the first computer invented in today's world. It won't work because the software is too outdated. I thought about all our electronic devices and how they are always getting software updates. So, I asked myself why? The answer was that the software either needs a fix because of a bug or can't keep up with the changes in the physical world. Then I realized that if everything that uses information needs to keep updating its software to function properly in the physical world, what about us? Don't we use information to run our lives? Aren't our brains programmed from information from our physical environments? Shouldn't we need updates to keep up with the changing world? We do, but we were never taught how to update our software or operating system. The difference between a device and us is that the device will accept the update without any resistance, but the brain acting through perception will fight to stay the same by trying to make our lives work with outdated software. So, how do we update our software? Devices have updates sent to them from whoever invented them, but we must see our updates in our physical experiences because our physical experiences created our operating system. Since God created us, he will send us updates through our physical experiences. We don't have to download them; we must let go of the old software we hold onto with our beliefs. Let me give you an example to help you understand what I'm talking about. For years, I feared going into a gas station if a gas tanker truck was there filling it up. That fear came from a childhood experience where my friend's house burned down, and someone said that the fire was caused by the water heater blowing up. That experience created an emotional reaction in my brain of fear of anything that could blow up. Because of that reaction, it took years before I would buy my wife a gas grill because I feared the propane tank blowing up. It was hard for me to catch that fear because it didn't show up as a thought but as an emotion. I didn't think about the experience I had as a child that put the fear there; I just felt the fear of it. Then, one day, I was in an experience where the gas tanker truck was filling up the gas station, and I needed some gas. Something says to me, go and see if the fear is real; go and see if the gas tanker truck blows up while you are pumping gas. That voice was God telling me to go into the gas station and get my software update for this experience saved as an emotional reaction. Remember that every physical experience must get its own update. So, I decided to go into the gas station because I would usually drive past the station and go to another. The gas tanker truck didn't blow up, and now that experience from my childhood is being updated with the truth. What's the truth? Gas tanker trucks don't blow up when filling gas stations. The more I did it, the less I feared it blowing up; until now, it doesn't bother me at all. Updating that fear through my physical experiences has allowed me to buy my wife a gas grill and go buy the propane tanks for it. To change our outdated software, which are emotional reactions in the brain, we must use our own physical experiences to see them. Reading about other people's lives is okay to see what they discovered that might help you. But until you go out into your own physical experiences and see your programming, you can't change it. The world is constantly changing. Are you updating your software or trying to make the world fit your perception? The brain runs our software program through emotional reactions and thoughts and can't update itself. It must react the same in all our physical experiences, but we don't. Meaning we can watch the programming instead of reacting to it. It will be hard initially because the program uses emotions and thoughts to get us to act. Practicing slowing our reaction to perception will change the brain at the mental and emotional levels.

THE BRAIN

Understanding Our Reference for Truth

When we are born, there is no reference for the truth in us, meaning we can't know if what we are being taught is true or not. To know the truth, we must know what a lie is, and because we come into the physical world without any information, we are at the mercy of our physical environments for truth. And because we all go through the same entry process, we are taught what the people who came before us were taught, who was taught by the people before them, and so on. Once we download enough information from our physical environments, that information becomes our reference for truth.

Our reference for truth is hard to catch because it appears as perception. Notice that the word perception has the prefix "pre" on it, which means before. Perception reacts to all our physical experiences, including those we think about before we act. Let me explain because it is essential if we want to get free from perception.

JOSE VILLEGAS

I grew up in an environment where breaking the law and getting over on each other was a way of life, so that became my reference for truth. Here's an example of how my reference for the truth played out in my life. The time had come for the sticker on my tags to be renewed, but I didn't have the money. So, I decided to go to the arts and crafts store and buy some paint to change the color and design of the expired tag sticker. I painted the sticker on my tags the same color as a new tag sticker and rode around that way for a while. Then, one day, the police pulled me over for the tag light being out. When he ran my license plate, it came back with expired tags. He gave me a $250 ticket and then removed the license plates from my car. I then had to have it towed to my house. Ultimately, it cost me almost 500 dollars, while renewing my tags only cost 135. I had to call around to some of my friends to borrow enough money to pay for the ticket and renew my tags. Why didn't I think of that in the beginning? My reference for truth in this situation is to be slick and break the law, and my brain could not act against itself by giving me another option. The brain will let you see other options only after you go the way it wants you to. Why didn't the brain release the thought of borrowing the 135 dollars from my friends as an option? Because that's not a part of my reference for the truth. My reference

THE BRAIN

is breaking the law and being slick. I realized that living through the brain as perception always costs more. Because of that experience with my tags, I learned my lesson and have never done it again, but I don't usually learn the truth in one lesson; some take a lifetime. But how did I come to this understanding about the reference for the truth? It was through a conversation I was having with someone, and I made the statement that as long as we as Human Beings keep living through perception, we will keep creating Hell on Earth. That person flat-out disagreed with me and said, this is not Hell. They went on to say that this world is going to end. I asked them how they knew that. They said because it is in the Bible; then I emphasized it again, but how do you know that is true? They said it's written in Revelations. I said I don't read Revelations because I don't want to put that idea into my brain. I also asked why work so hard for success to have a better life if all of it would end regardless. They did not have a response to that question. That's when it hit me: we can believe something to be true because it was taught as the truth without any evidence to prove that it's true. There's no way they could prove that the world would end while we are still here. But if enough people think and believe the same thing, we can make it true. Understanding your reference for truth is so important because you could be believing in something untrue. Like a crip shooting at blood because of their reference for truth. A gang member will have a different reference for truth than a church member. They both have the same commitment that their reference for truth is true. Reference for truth is controlled by our brains, which act as perception. That makes it hard for us to notice other truths in our experiences. It's not until we begin to work on separation from perception that we can see more truths in our own physical experiences. The only place to do this work is in our present-moment experiences because that's where the brain reacts to all our experiences, the ones that are physical and the ones we are just thinking about. Because I've done enough work to separate my spiritual self from my perception. I now see perception in action, even on television. I was watching this series on Netflix called "Fauda." This series is about Hamas and Israel and how two enemies live next to each other. However, what I noticed the most was each other's perception of each other, which is why this conflict has continued for so long. I don't want to get into that conflict, but not understanding your reference for truth can keep you stuck. As I'm watching the series, in one scene, one of the leaders of Hamas gets a call from the hotel manager to tell him that his cousin is there with another man. He got so mad that

THE BRAIN

I thought that he was going to kill her because she had sex out of wedlock. But what made him so mad? It was his reference for truth, which was the Koran. Stay with me because your brain is perceiving this and might make you mad and miss what I'm saying. I'm not saying anything negative about the Koran, but how the Hamas leader's brain was using it to justify his actions. Now, in the same episode, another scene shows him in a car with two other guys getting ready to leave a backpack with explosives at a bus stop. Not only did he blow up everybody at the bus stop, but he also blew up the guy who was carrying the backpack. After that scene, I said to myself he thought having sex out of wedlock was worse than blowing up innocent people at a bus stop. That's because his reference for the truth was coming from two places. One was the Koran, and the other was from his physical environment as a child. It is important to understand that he is not choosing what reference for truth he is using. His brain does it through perception. His brain used the Koran as the reference for truth to justify his anger at his cousin for having sex out of wedlock. It then justified blowing everybody up at the bus stop from the reference for the truth he downloaded from his physical environment. He was celebrated for blowing up innocent people at the bus stop. Everybody around him thought the same way, so how could he ever see any other truth? That's why the hotel manager called him; he believes the same way. Can you now understand why separating from perception is so important? You can have conflicting beliefs and believe they both are right.

THE BRAIN

The Spiritual Tool of Going into Awareness

The power of going into awareness when understood can result in significant changes in one's life. What is awareness and how is it used to change one's life? One of the definitions of awareness - is the state or ability to perceive, feel, or be conscious of events, objects, or sensory patterns. As I read through all the definitions of awareness, I found that they are defined as a state of consciousness. Defining it as only a state of consciousness still leaves out the one whose consciousness it is defining.

My definition of awareness takes it from a conscious state to a spiritual noun. I'm describing it as who we are spiritually. We spiritually are the consciousness or awareness that's aware of everything but our spiritual selves. The spiritual tool of going into awareness is deciding not to react but to observe the inner and outer movement for as long as possible. I call it a spiritual tool because of the word "going." That word implies that a decision must be made, and because of that, it is something we can use. It's also a spiritual tool because awareness is spiritual; it happens in the inner world. If it were a physical tool, I would have named it based on its function in the physical world. In the Bible, Psalm 46:10 says, "Be still, and know that I am God." For a long time, I thought that meant to be still to know God, but through practicing going into awareness, I realized that it meant to be still to know that we are God's. We are not the God who created everything, but we are the Gods of the physical world. You can see that we are the most powerful on the earth, but we do not rule over the earth, but rather each other. Which is creating Gods in conflict. Most of us have never been taught how to be still because no one knows what spiritual movement is. What is spiritual movement? It's to make a decision. The only spiritual move we can make as Beings is to make a decision. I know that sounds too simple, and many might miss it because of its simplicity. Spiritual movement happens every time we decide because all decisions occur in the spiritual world within us. There's never a time when we are not making a decision, but here's how we become spiritually still in our physical bodies. We must begin to practice making a decision not to react. We decide to stay in observation mode by not reacting to the negative feelings and thoughts that are stimulated by our

THE BRAIN

physical experiences. That doesn't mean our minds and emotions are not moving because they are, but we decide not to follow them by reacting to them. It's important to understand that nothing moves in your life without a decision. In the physical world, everything moves after a decision is made, but in the spiritual world, everything moves before a decision is made. In the spiritual world, it all happens in reverse. In the spiritual world, the voice of God, the mind, and emotions move first in reaction to our physical experiences, and we move last by making a decision. Not reacting can only stop you spiritually; it can't stop your mind, emotions, or God from reacting. And because they are moving, and you are not, you will become aware of them through observation. Spiritual stillness is staying in observation mode for as long as possible by slowing your reaction to your inner movement. We don't realize that every physical experience has a time or gap from when we observe it to when we react to it. Deciding to stay in observation mode widens that gap, and over time, it becomes easier to stay still. It's important to understand that everything in the inner world moves independently of each other. Think about the times when you felt an emotion that did not have a thought attached to it, but once you felt it, the mind jumped in by telling you a story about what it thinks is going to happen. Or other times when you had a thought about something without an emotion attached to it, but once you received the thought, the brain fired off an emotion that changed how you felt. What about when God spoke to you when you were not thinking or feeling anything noticeable? After you hear God, your mind reacts by trying to convince you to listen to it. So, what's our spiritual role in all of this? It's the decisions we make while all of it is happening. Who do we listen to or react to? Remember that everything else is moving, including God, and we can only watch everything moving by not moving ourselves. We stop our spiritual movement by deciding not to react. The more we practice staying spiritually still, the more we will trust the process and the more power we will have over our lives. Our families and friends will provide us with many opportunities to practice going into awareness. Below is a list of why going into awareness works. Practice as much as possible until it becomes a habit. Once it becomes a habit, you won't have to think about doing it anymore. It will become an unconscious act, and that's when the real magic happens.

THE BRAIN

Why Does Going into Awareness Work?

1. It's not an answer. It does not give us the answer we seek because it's just watching the movement of both worlds. It would have to give us a thought or idea to be an answer. The brain is in charge of that, and we are the observers of movement with the ability to make decisions. The brain is blocking our answers through perception. Going into awareness keeps us still by not reacting to perception, which allows the answer we need to show up.

2. It works because it's not another idea to live from as a concept in our heads. Looking at our lives, we will notice that we are living through some idea or concept about ourselves given to us as

children. Awareness will reveal that idea or concept so you can stop living through it unconsciously.

3. Going into awareness does not make anything right or wrong; it simply watches our inner movement. Our physical experiences will produce the revelation that will determine what's right or wrong for us.

4. Going into awareness allows our physical experiences to lead and not our minds or emotions. It's through our physical experiences that God communicates with us.

5. Practicing going into awareness does not take a side. It can't take a side because it's just watching the inner movement caused by our physical experiences. Living through perception is the only way to take a side in life. Awareness is watching our minds and emotions and learning what side they are on. When we become aware of what side our minds and emotions

are on, we can move away from it through awareness. The more we practice becoming aware of the movement of both worlds, the freer we will be within.

6. The spiritual tool of awareness does not require you to believe in it. Most of our spiritual teachings expect us to believe without any physical evidence. Awareness of the inner world, which is awareness of our minds, emotions, and God, is how we change our beliefs. Because most of us have never been taught how to be aware of our inner world, we ignore the physical evidence that what we believe is not working. How does one know when something is working or not? The evidence is in our physical lives. It was practicing going into awareness that I realized that most of us live disconnected from our own physical reality. Awareness will help us to reconnect with our physical reality and make the necessary changes.

7. Awareness is not thinking. It's hearing the mind talk and deciding not to make the same decision or not to make one at all. It allows you to see how things turn out.

8. Going into awareness is not emotional. We still feel the emotions produced by the brain, but let it happen and decide not to react in the same way.

9. Awareness is the original state in which we come into the physical world. That state has not gone anywhere; it's just not understood. We are always in observation, but usually, it's just focused on the physical world. Because it's focused on our physical experiences, we unconsciously react to the inner movement of our minds and emotions. And with the invention of texting, it's not even there anymore. People are walking around and driving in detachment from the physical world. As babies, we come into this world as observers, observing

THE BRAIN

everything moving outside us. This is how we learn, but the problem is that we are never taught about the one doing the observing. We are never taught that we are the quiet observer that lives within our bodies. We never realize that the one choosing the thought is us, not the thought we choose.

10. Awareness changes everything by allowing you to see what works and doesn't. Without awareness, we will keep making the same decisions even if they don't work because we don't know how to do anything else. These are some of the reasons why going into awareness works.

The Devil is in Us

What do I mean when I say that the devil is in us? What we call the devil is actually the brain, so it's in us.

First, let me say that I did not come up with this revelation. It was revealed to me because of the work I've done to separate myself from perception, which is controlled by the brain. By separating from my brain, I now see truths about how things move in my inner world that I hadn't noticed before. The brain operating through perception doesn't care about the truth. It only wants complete control over our lives. Doesn't that sound like the devil? It does that by reacting to all our physical experiences and even anything we think about before we act. Let me give you the physical experience that revealed this revelation to me. One day, I had some free time and decided that I would go to the gym. The moment I decided to go to the gym, my brain released chemicals into my body that made me feel like not wanting to go. I realized at that moment that I did not have that feeling before I had the thought of going to the gym. That's when I realized that the brain was not only reacting to my outer

THE BRAIN

physical experiences but also my inner thoughts before I acted on them. That's when I said to myself that it's my brain and not the devil trying to run my life all the time. I realized that if my brain is reacting to my thoughts before I make a decision, how can I ever have control of my life? I also realized that the battle for our lives is not fought between God and the devil but between perception and imagination, and the battlefield is physical reality. This is why we are suffering, hurting, and killing each other because the brain is telling us to do it. This revelation did not come from the brain but through practicing slowing my reaction down to perception. This revelation about the devil being the brain must be understood if we want to get better. I had reservations when I first understood this revelation before I wrote about it. The main reservation was how emotional people are about religion and that they might miss what I'm saying. As I wrote this, I realized that I couldn't control how other's brains would react to this truth about us. I didn't come up with this; I noticed it in my physical experiences. One of the main reasons we have created hell on earth is because we are living our lives from books and not our own physical experiences. It was a book that told us about a devil that we have never seen. Have you ever seen a man in a red suit with horns and a pitchfork? So, I decided to write about it anyway because too much is at stake for not knowing it. I can see us eventually having a nuclear war if we keep letting the brain run everything. A story I heard on the news pushed me into writing about this revelation. The story was about a young man who killed himself in a bathroom at an amusement park. He was at the amusement park to do a mass shooting. He was well-equipped with enough weapons and ammunition to hurt many people. But he decided to write on the wall of the bathroom, "I'm not a killer," before killing himself. When I heard that story, I realized that at some point in that experience, he knew he wasn't his mind or emotions but didn't know how to stop himself from acting out. So, he decided if he killed himself, he would not be able to hurt anyone. And that is what he did. Some will hear that story and think it was the devil, but it wasn't. It was his brain controlling him, and the only way to get liberation from it was through death. He didn't kill his spiritual self; he killed his brain. I bet that if you look at his past, his brain has always controlled him through anger. And he didn't know how to stop it. Think about all the stories of mass shootings and how they end. Most mass shooters usually either commit suicide or suicide by shooting it out with the police. Why is that? Because the same brain that convinced them to do it then turns around and tells them how crazy that was. And because the brain controls how we feel, it probably made

THE BRAIN

them feel so bad about what they had just done that they couldn't live with themselves anymore. It then tells them to kill themselves. That is why you find them with a self-inflicted gunshot wound in the woods somewhere by themselves. They are not alone but in bad company with the devil, their brains. Looking into the world today, I can see how the brain controls us all. But because we blame anything wrong on the devil, we will never be able to be spiritually free while here on earth, even if you don't believe me about this revelation. Go into your own physical experiences, work on separating from perception controlled by your brain, and see what you discover. How your brain controls you is based on how your physical environment developed it as a child. Remember that the battle for our physical lives is fought between perception and imagination and not God and the devil. The life you are now living is showing you who is winning. If your life is not changing, then perception is winning because perception operates from the past. If your life changes, imagination is winning because it operates in the future.

Be Nothing

We've been told to be something all our lives, and yet our power comes from realizing that spiritually, we are nothing. We are the "I am" of existence. In the bible, it says, "And who do they say I am?" tell them that I am that I am. If we are made in the spiritual image of God, then we are the I am, too. We say it but don't realize it.

When someone asks you what you do for a living, you always respond with, "I'm a doctor, I'm a lawyer, or I'm a truck driver. The "I'm" before what you do is the spiritual you. What I'm talking about is that spiritually, we are not what we do. Consciousness can't be the things it is observing. The problem is that consciousness can't be observed, so knowledge about it is hard to come by. So, we identify our consciousness with the things in the physical world as ourselves because the real self can't be experienced physically. Let's not confuse choosing a way of life with being nothing spiritually. We can choose to live as anything we want on Earth physically, but when we decide to change our physical expression, it's the spiritual you who's making that decision. That part is not what we change out of or into; it's the spiritual nothingness behind all our physical expressions. Spiritually, we play a lot of roles as we move throughout our day. Here's an example of what I'm talking about. One day, while standing in the kitchen, my daughter asked me a question. I spiritually move into the role of a father to give her the answer I think she needs. At that moment, my wife asked me something, and I switched from the role of a father to the role of a husband. While that was happening, my mother-in-law was over, and she started to talk to me; at that moment, I moved into the role of a son-in-law. The question I ask is, which one is me? Spiritually, none; I'm the one doing the switching, but I'm doing the switching seamlessly and unconsciously. What if, spiritually, I was one of those roles? Say, for example, that I was a father all the time. I would be talking to my wife and mother-in-law like a child, and you know that that won't work. What if, spiritually, I was a husband all the time? I would be talking to my daughter and mother-in-law as a spouse. Or what if, spiritually, I was a son-in-law all the time? I would interact with my wife and kids as a son-in-law. Role-playing happens all day and all the time until somebody wakes us from the ignorance created by information about us. That's what I'm doing, waking us up consciously. As babies, we spiritually enter the Earth as nothing, not as Christians, Muslims, Buddhists, Crips or Bloods, Democrats or Republicans, just babies. We are so free that we don't even have a name. Then, we are cultivated into a world of thinking where information about us is left out or unknown. Then, we identify our spiritual selves with the roles we play. And when we do that, it puts us on a side mentally and emotionally that we must defend and protect to our last dying breath. If we came into the physical world spiritually as something, we would only be able to experience the physical world one way. We wouldn't be called human beings anymore, just animals. We had to come into the physical world spiritually as nothing to express ourselves as everything. God could not create us spiritually as something because we would not be free. Every other animal and thing comes into the physical world as something, so they can't be anything else. When I use the word "nothing," I'm not talking about being powerless but having all power on the Earth. The nothing I'm talking about is being "no-thing," nothing physical. How can we spiritually be anything that's already here before we enter the physical world through our bodies? The reason it's so hard not to identify with our physical expressions as our spiritual selves is that we can't experience our spiritual selves with our five senses; we can only know that we spiritually exist; we can't experience our spiritual selves as spiritual. What's

THE BRAIN

the power in understanding this truth about us? It will allow us to quietly live in the moment behind our titles and spiritual names but know that they are not who we are. Living quietly behind our titles and spiritual names as spiritual nothingness tends to lend more flexibility to our physical experiences. We stop fussing and fighting over ideas because of who we think we are but let some stuff go because of who we know we are. Living in our physical experiences as the titles and spiritual names tends to make us rigid and close-minded. That causes us to have negative inner reactions that we think are generated from the outside in. But our attachment to the titles and spiritual names as our spiritual selves is the cause of our negative inner reactions. So, whatever you decide to be in the physical world, remember that behind the physical expression you choose, spiritually, you are nothing.

JOSE VILLEGAS

We are the Created Creators

Say that title to yourself repeatedly until you feel that truth burst within your understanding. We are the created Creators. We have been created to create.

If we look at that statement from a purely physical point of view, we will see it. Our physical bodies have been made to move and build whatever we think. Other species can climb, run, swim, and crawl, but can they create? Can they build something in the air, on the land, or beneath the seas? Can they look at a problem and come up with a solution? No, they can't because they were not created to be Creators. We can look at a situation and devise a way to make it work or create a new way. We can do surgery on any part of our bodies, including our hearts and brains. What animal can do that? We have built tunnels underwater without draining the river. We have flown to the moon and landed like an airplane on the return trip. We've connected the whole world through the internet, and this is just the physical attributes. What about our mental attributes? We can think,

THE BRAIN

reason, and contemplate. We can notice and hear our thoughts and become aware of our feelings. We can receive thoughts and transmit them back into the Universe through imagination. We can build our lives into something great or live in total defeat. We were created to be Creators and must come to realize this truth to take our rightful place as heirs of the power of God on Earth. We have been created to rule over the things on the Earth. We are lower than the Creator of everything but higher than everything made on the Earth. Our power is limited to the physical world. If all of this is true, then why are we not ruling over the things on the Earth? We are ruling over the things on the Earth, but we are doing it through ignorance. We are trying to control the Earth through thinking, and thinking alone is dangerous. Thinking is a part of the creative process, but thinking alone leads to insanity. Why does thinking lead to insanity? It leaves out four other parts of the creating process. It leaves out our physical experiences that must lead, God, our emotions, and us as observers and decision-makers. So, all together, including the mind, makes five parts to the creating process. To create, we must understand the relationship between these five parts of our lives. Out of all of them, the most important part is our physical experiences. Why didn't I put God first because God talks to us through our physical experiences?

How many people do you know that love God but live through perception, and their lives are still in ruins? Our physical experiences are the center of life, where everything happens. They activate the voice of God, our minds, and our emotions. Why don't we know this since that's how we create? As the created Creators, we come into the physical world in ignorance, so if this information is not being taught, you won't know it. Out of all the teachings I have been involved in, none has taught about how to create. Most of it is about trying to know God, not us as the created Creators. If we want to know God, we must understand ourselves more. It's our spiritual and physical responsibility to run the physical world. Who or what else has been created to do it if not us? We cannot "Not Create," meaning we are constantly creating through our decisions and actions. So, if we are continually creating, we at least need to know how. We can avoid the responsibility of creating our own physical lives, but we can't avoid the pain of what we've created unconsciously. The physical world is the canvas of life; what we paint on it as our physical lives are the brushstrokes of all our decisions. Start creating a better life for yourself, and all else will be okay. It may mean returning to school or getting out of a bad relationship, starting to change what's right in front of you, and creating from there.

THE BRAIN

No Spiritual Order

I thought about why I wasn't physically benefiting from all the spiritual information I had acquired. And something told me that there isn't any order or sequence to our spiritual growth. Just like there's one for physical growth, there isn't one for spiritual growth. Look at how we learn and grow physically. We don't go from the 1st to the 12th grade. There's a process or sequence of learning that takes us from one level of learning to the next. That process is not found in the spiritual world. Our spiritual understanding usually starts with whatever book of the Bible our parents, or the Pastor taught us from as a child. If they are teaching from Hebrews, then our spiritual understanding started with Hebrews. Remember that when we are born, all our information must first come from the physical world, including our spiritual information. For most of us, our spiritual education came through some form of religion. And yet, we never start with the spiritual part of us, which is the Soul. If you look up the definition of Soul, it is defined as "the spiritual part of a person." My spiritual understanding did not start with that definition of Soul; it began with Hebrews. I can't remember ever being taught anything about me being a Soul. I was taught the principles from the bible as a child without any understanding of myself in the process. It's like being taught college material when we are in the first grade spiritually. So, I held ignorance against myself as if I could have known better. I grew up in an undisciplined environment where principles were for other people. If I had to write up a sequence for spiritual growth, this is where I would start.

1. First, I would teach about us as Souls that live within our bodies and are the only ones on the Earth with free "Will." And that we are the highest creation that God has created on Earth.

2. I would teach about the importance of the body and that it's the doorway into the physical world. I would teach that the spiritual and physical worlds need each other. Without the body, the soul would not have a place to stay on earth. Without the Soul, the body would not have any ideas.

THE BRAIN

3. I would teach what it means to be a Human Being and how to live in both worlds simultaneously as a Soul.

4. I would teach about the brain and how it projects past information into the present moment. I would teach that we are not the brain but must use it to create on the Earth. I would also teach how it is developed and how it comes into power over our lives.

5. I would teach that we must stop trying to force the higher principles on ourselves and that they are already working in our lives. If you break a spiritual principle, you will pay the consequences while here on Earth, and the same is true if you follow them; you will be rewarded.

6. I would teach about the power of awareness and how it helps us to see perception. If we can see it, we can't be it.

7. I would teach that pain is an indicator, not an enemy. It's trying to show us what we are not seeing about ourselves. But everywhere we go, we are taught to have joy, which is usually an avoidance of pain that makes us one-sided emotionally.

8. I would teach that the Soul is the only Creator on the Earth.

9. I would teach that everything has a spiritual foundation, and we have the power to move in the spirit of things. We move into the spirit of things through imagination. This is how we either attract what we want or push it away.

10. I would teach that we, as Souls, are information-dependent. This means that everything we learn must come from the physical world first. And because it came from somebody else, we should never stop seeking new information. What if they got it wrong?

THE BRAIN

11. I would teach how to live instinctively. Living instinctively is not just about listening to God's unemotional voice but also about becoming watchful of both worlds simultaneously by watching your feelings and the experiences that generate those feelings. This is hard because we have learned to react and not watch our feelings.

12. I would teach that as Souls, we must un-title ourselves. Stop calling ourselves the groups we belong to. How can we be anything when everything was already here before we were born? As living Souls, we don't have a physical identity; we are spiritually neutral. But we can take a physical side.

13. I would teach that we must live from our childlike nature to realize that we are already in the kingdom of Heaven within us. Think about how free you would become on the insides when you recreate your child-like states as an adult. Non-

judgment, unconditional love, neutrality, and being present in the present moment are some of the child-like states. Those states are how we realize that we are already in the kingdom of Heaven within us. Heaven is just another name for the spiritual world. Because we are in a body and the body creates an inner world, that world is spiritual. You don't have to die to go to Heaven, but you can live from it while you are still alive and on Earth. I'm living from mine, and I can see how wonderful it is. How do we get there? By freeing our Souls or "Beings" from our "Human" side. The brain runs the "Human," so if we separate from the brain by not reacting to it constantly, it will separate us from the "Human." The Soul or "Being" part of us is in the kingdom already, but we don't know it. I would begin to teach about the spiritual world in the order above. Can you see why the order of learning is so important? Without it, significant information will be

THE BRAIN

missed. I've read many spiritual books and still have not found a spiritual order of learning. No one is teaching how to go from one level to the next. No order leads to slow and painful growth.

The Physical World

The physical world is very important, even if we don't respect it. Without the physical world, we could not exist as separate Beings because the Human or body would not exist. Without the physical world, where would we create? There's no space in the spiritual world to create because everything is one unified mass of energy. That's why the physical world was formed, so the spiritual world had a place to create.

If the physical world did not exist, we would not have any emotions because our brains control them, and our physical experiences develop our brains. Without the physical world, we wouldn't have a developed mind or a mind at all. Without the physical world, spiritual revelations would not be possible because we wouldn't have any physical experiences where revelations happen. I know I've started just about every sentence with the words "without the physical world," but it's so important that we understand the physical world's role in our spiritual existence. How would you know one "Being" from another if not for our physical bodies? The physical world is so important that God created

THE BRAIN

it before he created us. It's still happening today; every time a newborn comes into this world, their physical body must be developed first. All the wars are fought over land, which is part of the physical world. I don't know what you were taught about the physical world, but I was taught to reject and condemn it. They taught me that I was just passing through this is not my home. It still amazes me how we say that somebody is in a better place when they die, but nobody is trying to die to go there. We all are still trying to hold on to this physical life for as long as possible because it's the only world we can know about through our senses. The problem with learning about the physical and the spiritual worlds is that we teach them separately; it's never taught in unity. The physical world is left up to the Scientist, and the spiritual world is left to the Priests and the Pastors. And yet we live in both worlds at the same time; that's why we are called Human Beings. If they came together, they would realize that they need each other. It is now time to unify both worlds so that we can have power in our own physical lives. We spend so much time teaching about where we are going once our bodies die that we forget to teach about how to live in them. Nobody truly knows what's going to happen when they die because you must die to answer that question. We cannot answer a dying question while we are still alive and in our bodies. The spiritual part of us never dies because we cannot kill energy; it can only be transformed. Who knows, we may immediately get into the body of a newborn baby; who knows? And if we take on another body, we will not remember that we were here because with a new body comes an undeveloped brain. So, stop beating up on the physical world and embrace its importance.

THE BRAIN

Pain is a Gift

Pain is a gift that nobody wants. It's a gift because it's the only thing strong enough to produce change. It's the only thing that will make you think about what you are doing to yourself.

All my life, it was implied that pain was the enemy. That pain was of the devil, and I should pray and worship it away. Because of practicing living in the moment, I have come to realize what a great gift pain is. If it were not for pain, I would not have changed to receive this level of understanding. Life uses pain to wake us up, but we are taught to stay asleep by avoiding it or blaming it on the devil. If we are in pain, it is trying to show us something about ourselves that we can't see in the area that the pain is in. Pain is the balancing force of joy. To always want to be happy is consumed with the idea of joy, which is to be one-sided. I don't welcome pain, and I don't seek joy at the exclusion of pain. I let life happen, and as a result, I experience many emotions. Pain just happens to be one of them. When pain shows up in my life, I know it's time to grow in the area that it showed up in. When I was running around trying to be nice to everybody as a way of compensating for self-hatred, pain showed up in that area. As long as I tried to avoid the pain, it kept me in pain in that area. Our whole life is not full of pain; it is just the areas in which we need some work. Pain is not an enemy but a friend of ours because without it, we would destroy ourselves with pleasure. Don't avoid your pain but ask yourself what it is trying to show me about myself that I don't know. When you question yourself in this way, it helps you to understand that it's something you are doing that is causing it. Pain is necessary, but suffering is optional. Optional means that we can learn from the first few painful situations or suffer because of lessons not learned. I know it will be hard to accept pain as a gift when all our lives we have done everything to avoid it. Avoiding it is why we have not grown into an awareness of ourselves. Life uses pain to initiate the answers we are looking for. So don't avoid your pain, but become aware of it when you are in it. And don't use anything not to feel it, so you can learn from it. Remember, pain is a gift nobody wants.

THE BRAIN

His Answers

This title came to me as I watched a Pastor preach on TV. He told his story about how God spoke to him to tithe 500 dollars, and he only had $503.00 in the bank. And he went on to tell how things turned around in his life.

A year earlier, I was watching this same program with a different Pastor, and he told a similar story. At the end of his talk, he asked 300 people to send in a $1000.00 seed, and in 90 days, we would get it back 10-fold. At that moment, I had 1175.00 dollars in the bank. So, I wrote a check for 1000.00 dollars and sent it in. For three days, I went in and out of mental and emotional struggle about if I did the right thing. I even thought about canceling the check, but I didn't. I still haven't gotten back 1-fold, let alone 10-fold. Please understand me. I'm not saying tithing works or doesn't work. I'm saying that if it's not your answer spoken directly to you, then it may not work for you. But I did get an answer that was worth more than anything money could buy. It cost me 1,000 dollars for this priceless wisdom. That wisdom is that we cannot do what somebody else did and expect the same results.

Why is that? Because what he did was his answer for his life at that moment in time for his stage of spiritual development. The Pastor was told to give $500, and I couldn't have known at what stage of his spiritual growth that was his next answer. His goal was to become a Pastor, and tithing was part of that journey. Looking back at where I was when I gave, I did it out of desperation, not revelation. My financial condition was one of pain and suffering. I was trying to manipulate God into moving on my behalf for 1000 dollars. The Pastor's internal state may have been ready for this level of giving, but mine wasn't. I should not have given because I had already scared whatever I gave with desperation. Pain attached to my giving created an unconscious need for a return on one's investment. What I'm trying to get us to understand is that everyone must get their own answers. And those answers must come through their own physical experiences. The problem when we follow others is that they can't have our answers because they can't know what answers we need and when we need them. There is no such thing as one answer that fits all because everyone is different and may need a different answer. We may even need the same answer but at a different time in our lives. Nobody is teaching us how to get answers from our own physical experiences because they don't know how. They are teaching us what worked for them, but that

THE BRAIN

doesn't mean it will work for you. Some of the stuff may work, but more than likely, most of it won't because it's not your answer but his answer. How can we have our own answers when we come into the physical world in total ignorance? That 1000 dollars I gave earlier gave me back this wisdom, which is priceless. Stop looking for answers and learn to be aware of them when they appear in your physical experiences.

Where are Our Answers?

They are in our own physical experiences. Our physical experiences are the only place where God communicates with us. Even when we go somewhere, we are still in a physical experience.

It became apparent that we are not taught to look to our own physical experiences for answers. We are taught that we must go somewhere to get them. What do we do when we leave those places we went to get answers? Do we know how to get our own answers when not in a group environment? Before Moses went to the Red Sea, he did not go there with the answers for what to do next. He did not have a group to attend where he could float the question to find an answer about what might happen when he arrived. He went to the Red Sea to "See" what to do next. Now, this next part is essential and a significant key to freedom on Earth. Now, if God is all-knowing and knows everything, wouldn't he have known that the Red Sea needed to be parted? Yes, he did. Why didn't he part it before Moses got there? Stay with me because this is so powerful that

THE BRAIN

I shouted when God spoke it. I heard God say to me that I didn't do it before he got there because Moses wasn't in the physical experience where that was needed as an answer. Moses needed to be in the physical experience where the Sea needed to be parted for God to release that as an answer. What if Moses had decided he wasn't going to go to the Red Sea? Then, that as an answer would not have shown up in his life. I don't know if God split the Red Sea because I wasn't in that experience to see it. But I'm using it as an example to teach us something about us, God, and our physical experiences. We must understand that two things must come together for God to release an answer. You must be in the physical experience to get the answer you need. That's why going places to get answers before they are needed usually doesn't work because you are not in the physical experience where the answer is required. I'm not saying stop doing anything that is helping you change your life. Because I needed to go to my NA meetings when I stopped smoking crack. I'm saying to switch from group mode to present-moment awareness. Usually, all the information we picked up from the groups doesn't show up when needed. Because when we are in the physical experience where we need an answer, we are usually very reactive, so the answer can't appear. How often have you noticed the other ways you could have acted after reacting? But I don't have to go to such a big answer as parting the Red Sea to show you that the answer is always there when we are in a physical experience where one is needed. I can show you a smaller answer, but still an answer. The size of the answer doesn't matter. What matters is that the answer is always there when needed. One day, while walking through the grocery store shopping, I heard something say to me get some eggs. I didn't hear that voice until I passed by the eggs. I didn't hear it when I walked down the bread aisle or through the meat section. I heard it when the eggs and I were in the same place. At that moment, my mind reacted and said, "You don't need any eggs," so I didn't buy any. We don't have to listen to that voice of God, but we do have to listen to something. It's usually the mind. When I got home and began to prepare some pancakes, the only thing I needed was what I didn't have. You guessed it, eggs. I didn't get mad; I was actually glad because I knew who said to get some eggs. Isn't that the same God that parted the Red Sea? Yes, it is, and he has always talked to every one of us directly. From that moment on, I started practicing listening and not just hearing. Listening is doing what it says, and hearing is hearing and debating what it says. If there were only one thing out of this chapter I would want you to hold on to, it would be to look to your own physical experiences for your answers. This is why nobody can have

THE BRAIN

your answer; because you must be in the physical experience where the answer is needed. Others can only give you information; they can't give you answers. It's so important that we get this because we have gotten it backward. We are trying to move God on our behalf with a lot of spiritual activity because we are not taught what moves God. God responds to our physical experiences to help us to get to the next physical experience. What blocks us is living through perception.

JOSE VILLEGAS

We Bring Consciousness to the Physical World

The physical world cannot be conscious or aware of itself. A tree doesn't know that it's a tree. A flower doesn't understand that it's a flower. Animals can't be aware of themselves in relationship to the physical world. They can only sense danger. They can't eliminate it from their environment.

All this started coming to me as I watched a TV show called Swamp People. As I watched them catch alligators, I realized that the alligators kept falling for the same old trick. It became clear to me that the alligator's level of consciousness or understanding was restricted to being an alligator. They did not understand that a piece of meat on a rope hanging from a tree was a trap. It also meant that they didn't communicate danger to each other. If they did, other alligators could avoid being caught, and the pocketbook and shoe business would not exist. The Deer is still getting hit on the highway. You would think by now that it would know how to cross the street. They are still getting hit because they are not conscious of the whole world, just their world. I went on a field trip to Luray Caverns with my younger daughter. As I was walking through the caverns, I realized that I could comprehend beauty. I don't think any other animal can understand life the way we can. We bring consciousness or awareness to the physical world. What do I mean when I say we bring consciousness to the physical world? I mean that beauty can't be aware of itself. It can't say this is beautiful and that it is not. Sound can't hear itself and say to itself that sounds good, and that sounds bad. Love can't be expressed without us being aware of what love is. Evil could not exist on the Earth without us doing it. We have been given the ability to be aware of the whole world in relationship to ourselves. We also bring awareness and consciousness to each other. Would you care as much about your appearance if there wasn't anyone here to see it? Without someone to be aware of us, how would we know ourselves or change our lives? That's why discussing our problems and personal discoveries helps us better understand ourselves. All self-help groups are built upon this understanding. When we talk about our lives openly with each other, it makes us more aware of our own lives. It can also work in reverse, where we worry about what others think of us, so we don't talk openly about ourselves. So, remember that we need each other to see ourselves.

THE BRAIN

We Can't Know What's Going To Happen Next

We can't know and are not supposed to know what will happen next. We have been created only to know what has happened and what is happening. Even what has happened is a function of perception, and it's the brain's job to remind us of it in the present moment.

Not knowing what will happen next is not a lie or some game we are playing with ourselves. It's the truth about all of us, and no one can know what will happen next before it happens. How many times has someone started predicting that the world is coming to an end? And yet, we are still here. We never question the predictors because we believe it's true, even if it has never happened. We must go into our physical experiences fresh and open and let the experience tell us what to do next. We must understand that we can't know something before it happens. We can only think and believe that we do. The thinking and feeling that we know what's going to happen next keeps us stuck in the prison of perception. True freedom is living on the edge of our physical experiences with the understanding that we don't know what's going to happen next. It may seem scary to be out there, but that's where our true power lies. Our power comes from not being controlled by our minds and emotions but coexisting with them as Observers. An Observer is simply the state we are in as Creators when we are not reacting. It requires being comfortable with uncertainty when most of us want certainty, but with practice, it gets easier. Do you know how much mental and emotional pain you would be in if you knew what was going to happen next before it happened? What if you knew today everything that would happen for the next 30 days before it happened? You could only know it. You couldn't change it because it hasn't happened yet. How would that affect you mentally and emotionally? It would drive you crazy trying to change it before it happened. What if, on day 17, you saw yourself in a bad car accident but could not change that event but could only know when it would happen? How would you handle that knowledge? That knowledge would drive you insane. I know on day 17, you would not drive or get in a car, but that would not stop it because it must happen. Now, can you see why I'm glad we can only know the past and experience the present moment? We may want to know, but we can't

THE BRAIN

know because we are not supposed to know. But because we want to know, it causes us to listen to what our minds think will happen. And because the mind can't know either, we recreate our past in the present moment. We waste too much time talking about things we think we know but can't know and are not supposed to know. We need to spend more time practicing living in the moment in observation mode to become more aware of the guidance in our physical experiences.

Things to Remember

1. "I don't know what's going to happen next" is a powerful truth. Say it to yourself throughout the day. You may say it out loud or think it quietly to yourself.

2. If you knew what was going to happen next before it happened, it would drive you crazy. Not knowing what will happen next is God's way of keeping us sane.

3. The mind wants to know, so it makes up stories based on what it thinks will happen next. If you believe the story and decide from it, you will have a past life in the present moment.

4. Not knowing what will happen next keeps us in the moment.

THE BRAIN

5. God is in the moment, and so are we. God will let us know if we need to know something before it happens. That voice we call "something said" is God talking to us.

Things We Should Know about Emotions

1. We can't stay satisfied emotionally in the physical world. Let's not confuse being happy with being satisfied. Being happy lasts as long as the emotion that caused it, and being satisfied is trying to keep that same feeling all the time. When we experience getting something we want, we are experiencing it at its highest emotional level. Once experienced, the emotion begins to return to its normal level. That's why we keep buying more and bigger in an attempt to stay emotionally satisfied. We don't understand that how we feel about something is not controlled by us but by our brains. We usually fall into what I call "recapture," where we try to recapture a feeling we had in

THE BRAIN

a previous experience. The word satisfaction is tied to our emotions. It's a feeling word. How do you feel about that new car now that some time has passed? What about that new house or that fresh and exciting new relationship? I'm trying to get us to see that we are here to experience life, not to control what we feel all the time. If you want satisfaction, start allowing yourself to experience the full array of emotions. The more we allow ourselves to experience all our feelings, the more balanced we will become emotionally. We will create what I call a new emotional normal. A new emotional normal is where we are not constantly going bipolar but become more emotionally buoyant in our lives. We don't do this with effort. It happens automatically. We must allow it to happen by becoming more willing to feel all of our emotions. I would probably be dead or in jail if it were not for pain. And because many of us view pain through the understanding of being bad, we either avoid it or rush to change it. We never learn from it. We have lived so long in ignorance about our emotions that they have quietly taken over our lives. Something as simple as knowing that our brains control how we feel emotionally is not taught anywhere. Understanding that the brain controls how I feel emotionally has helped me to live my life differently. First, it made me realize that I was reacting to an emotion that was generated by my brain.

2. Secondly, it made me realize that the physical world could not keep me satisfied emotionally because my brain was consistently firing off different chemicals.

3. Thirdly, I realized that whatever I accomplished would become emotionally normal sooner or later. If everything becomes emotionally normal sooner or later, why not experience every experience individually? Say you went out on

a date and had a great time. Don't try to recreate that experience emotionally. Just let it happen.

Things to Remember

1. All emotional reactions to our physical experiences do not come from us. It's coming from the brain. How can we be the emotion and feel it, too?

2. Practice emotional discovery. Emotional discovery involves going into an experience to see how it feels. It is not about being strong or weak. It's about learning about your life at the emotional level. If you are always saying yes, go and see how "no" feels.

3. Stop living in emotional anticipation. Emotional anticipation is anticipating how you will feel before you have a physical experience. How can you know how you will feel before something happens, you can't? You can't know what chemicals your

THE BRAIN

brain will fire off in response to the experience.

4. Our brains take sides in our lives emotionally. This came to me as the result of noticing how I was feeling watching a show on cheating spouses. I noticed that when the guys cheated, I didn't feel anger, but when the women did it, I noticed a negative emotional reaction inside of me. The fact that I noticed it is because of the work I've done separating myself from perception in the present moment. When we start to notice our inner emotional reactions before we act, we move into mastering our own lives.

5. Every physical experience generates its own emotion. Not knowing this can cause us to live in physical contradictions. Here's an example of how I came about this physical revelation. One day, while driving to work, another driver in my lane made a no-left turn during rush hour. It backed up the lane quickly, so I started

cursing him out. As I was ranting and raving, something said to me, didn't you make that same turn earlier in the week? At that moment, I broke out in a laugh. And that's when I realized that every physical experience generates its own emotions. The emotion I felt when I made the illegal turn wasn't the same emotion I felt when somebody else did it. Understanding this has helped me give others and myself a break from reacting so quickly.

6. We don't get to choose our addictions; they are chosen for us by our brains. We don't come into the physical world with likes and dislikes. Our brains determine all of them. I watched a show called "Bizarre Food" where kids were eating bugs like we eat popcorn. That's when I realized that our physical environment, not us, cultivates our likes and dislikes. Even the people we like must be okayed by our brains, not us. The brain will either make us feel good

about them or not, but either way, it's not our choice.

7. We must talk about how something feels after we do it to know that it's stopped working at the emotional level. It's important to understand how we are feeling before we do something. But usually, that doesn't prevent us from doing it. But talking about how it felt after we did it leaves a more profound impression on our consciousness. I've had times when I was getting ready to do something, and because I had been talking about how it felt after I did it the last time, I decided not to do it. Remembering how something felt the last time you did it before you do it, will help you to stop doing it because everything we do is about trying to feel good. We are addicted to feeling good. So, if something I'm doing to feel good is not making me feel good after I do it, I will eventually stop doing it.

8. Stop trying not to be where you are emotionally. Say you say something stupid; don't try and do something else not to feel that feeling. Let more of the experience play out, and you will know what to do next. The more we allow ourselves to be where we are emotionally, the freer we will be spiritually.

9. We can't stop our emotions from happening. We can only stop ourselves from reacting too quickly. Because we don't understand this truth, we will try to control all our physical experiences and still end up unsatisfied.

THE BRAIN

Separation Talk

What is separation talk? It's talking in a way that creates separation from our minds and emotions. Here's what it sounds like. Say I want to talk about an experience I heard about but wasn't there. Here's how I would start my conversation off with. "I don't know if this is true, but this is what I heard." Starting off in that way creates separation from your mind.

The mind loves it when we talk about things we heard about as if we were there and knew it. The more you catch yourself speaking in a knowing about something you don't know, it will stop you from talking a lot. Here's another one of my favorites. Say someone says something to me, and I have a negative inner reaction. Here's how I would tell someone about it. "I don't know if this is true, but this is how I felt" when so and so say that. When I say it that way, it opens the door of understanding by making me realize it's an inner reaction. Just because I felt a certain way about something doesn't mean that it is true. Remember that our physical experiences must go through the filter of perception that's controlled by the brain first. We must realize that we are not giving ourselves those feelings and thoughts; it's our brains reacting to our physical experiences. This is why we must practice separation talk when talking to others. Talking to others about things we heard or read about as if we were there keeps us attached to our brains, which operates as perception in our lives. When I say, "I don't know if this is true, but this is how I felt," allows me more present-moment flexibility. I don't have to be rigid and closed-minded by attaching myself to a feeling that I did not give myself. It's also important to understand that talking this way detaches us from our emotions in a way that allows us to feel them still but not react too quickly. If we begin to notice how we talk about things, we will soon realize that we speak a lot about things we don't know, especially when we are talking about what another person is thinking. How can we know what somebody else is thinking? To know that we would have to be inside their body with them, and that's impossible.

THE BRAIN

Where Would I Start?

If there were one step I would practice, it would be "Let's just wait and see." The power of "Let's Just Wait and See" is that it lets our physical experiences lead. By letting our physical experiences lead and not perception. We will become more aware of ourselves as Creators with the power to create from what we see, not think.

Thinking is a function of the Creator. A Creator who lives through thinking alone is controlled by their mind. This is not about being intelligent or uneducated. It's about being manipulated by one of our most powerful abilities, thinking. Practicing "Let's just wait and see" doesn't fight against our minds or emotions. It allows them to express themselves, and we co-exist with them by waiting and not reacting. It also takes care of being responsible for being present in the present moment. If we are not reacting, then we are more present in the present moment. Practicing "Let's just wait and see" will grow us like a flower so we can stop trying to grow ourselves. And one of the most powerful revelations "Let's just wait and see" has given me is that we don't have to come up with our own answers. And that the only place to get those answers is inside our own physical experiences. How many years have we suffered because we did not know how to live inside of our own physical experiences? "Let's just wait and see" takes care of that by allowing us to get the answers we need when they are needed. The more we get our answers from our own physical experiences, the more we will practice "Let's just wait and see." "Let's just wait and see" is the foundation of what I practice that keeps me present in the present moment.

THE BRAIN

Why is all of this Important?

It's important because it's time to understand ourselves in relationship to everything else. We are the most powerful entity on the Earth and, as such, must move into our headship of the physical world.

This book is not about power over others but power over our own lives. To have power over one's own life, there must be separation from our minds and emotions, operating as perception. The new world order will not be another attempt at changing the outer world but living from the inner world. Living from the inner world will create a new world order in the outer world. Each and every one of us will become the Kings and Queens of our own inner world where only we reside. The beautiful thing about the inner world is that the outer world can't destroy it. The only way the outer world can keep us suffering is by following it more than the inner world. Once we give up the feeling of needing the outer world to be whole, we will realize that all our needs are met. And that's when we will become powerful in our own lives. We don't have to figure life out by ourselves. There is a power of intelligence that runs the whole world. It does not matter what you call this power; just get in touch with it and allow it to guide you. Our minds cannot lead us to inner freedom because it's a part of our inner movement that we must separate from to have freedom. Our minds will try to be this intelligence, but it can't because our physical environments developed it, so it's limited in knowledge. This power or intelligence that created the whole world knows everything, and it's the only thing that can know us. All of this is important because it's the next step in our evolution to become God's of our own physical lives. When I say God's over our own physical lives, I'm talking about ruling and creating from within our own spiritual world. The time has come for us to understand our spiritual selves. We can't just read about our power and have power without going out into our physical environments and cultivating it. Once we become powerful in our own lives, we can't lose it because it's who we are.

Conclusion

In conclusion, what I've discovered about myself has led to me understanding us as Human Beings. The world can't get better until we do. And because we live our lives through perception and don't know it, we are creating hell on Earth. Perception doesn't have our future in it because it operates out of the past. The goal is to practice separation from perception in the present moment by slowing your reactions down to what you feel and think. We have only two places to decide from: the present moment or perception. Choosing from perception is living from the past. Choosing from the present moment is going towards the future. Perception will allow you to have a head full of concepts and a life full of contradictions. Stay committed to the process I have outlined in "How to Change the Brain" until it becomes a habit, and then watch the habit change your brain. And remember, stop waiting on God because you have everything you need to change your life. Go out and become God on Earth.

Thanks, Jose V.

Made in the USA
Middletown, DE
01 September 2024